Ollscoil na hÉireann
National University of Ireland

The Irish State and the Diaspora

The 33rd O'Donnell Lecture 2008
An 33 Léacht Uí Dhónaill 2008

delivered at University College Dublin
(William Jefferson Clinton Institute)
tugtha in An Coláiste Ollscoile, Baile Átha Cliath
(i Halla Éisteachta William Jefferson Clinton)

by
le

Professor Mary E. Daly, MA, DPhil

Tuesday 18 November 2008
Dé Máirt 18 Samhain 2008

(as part of the NUI Centenary Celebrations)

49 Merrion Square Dublin 2 T: (+353 1) 439 2424 F: (+353 1) 439 2466
registrar@nui.ie www.nui.ie

O'Donnell Lecture 2008 (33rd in the series)
Léacht Uí Dhónaill 2008 (an 33 léacht san sraith)

The Irish State and the Diaspora

Cover image:
Emigrants At Cobh by Joseph Wilson
Reproduced by kind permission of the Wilson Family

Design and layout by
Brian Kelly Design Associates

ISSN: 1393-9726

ISBN: 978-0-901510-53-2

Price €10

O'DONNELL LECTURES

Charles James O'Donnell, born in Donegal and educated in Galway, provided in his will (1935) for a bequest to each of the Universities of Oxford, Wales, Edinburgh, National University of Ireland and Trinity College, to establish an annual lecture in each of the institutions – the lecture in the National University of Ireland to be on the history of Ireland since the time of Cromwell, with particular reference to the histories, since 1641, of old Irish families.

The NUI lecture series was established in 1957 and continued until 1986. Due to a lack of fund, there was a gap of some year, but the NUI Senate was pleased to be able to revive the series, to be presented annually in each of the NUI Constituent Universities in rotation, as and from 1999.

The O'Donnell Lecture 1999, the 28th in the series, was also the first O'Donnell Lecture to be delivered at the National University of Ireland, Maynooth. The 29th Lecture was delivered by Professor J.J. Lee in University College Cork, the 30th by Professor Tom Bartlett of University College Dublin and the 31st by Dáibhí Ó Cróinín in National University of Ireland, Galway. In 2004 the 32nd Lecture was delivered by Thomas O'Connor in National University of Ireland, Maynooth. This 33rd Lecture was delivered in University College Dublin as part of the NUI Programme of Events to celebrate the NUI Centenary in 2008.

PROFESSOR MARY E. DALY

Mary E. Daly is a Professor of History at University College Dublin, and Principal of the College of Arts and Celtic Studies. She studied for a BA and MA at UCD. In 1971 she was awarded the NUI Travelling Studentship in History and a Research Studentship at Nuffield College Oxford, where she obtained a DPhil. She is a member of the Royal Irish Academy (Secretary 2000-4) and the Higher Education Authority, and a former member of the National Archives Advisory Council and the Irish Manuscripts Commission.

She is the author of nine books and editor of four books on 19th and 20th century Ireland, most recently *The Slow Failure: Population Decline and Independent Ireland, 1920-1973* (Madison Wisconsin 2006), and *1916 in 1966,* (Dublin 2007), co-edited with Margaret O'Callaghan.

The Irish State and the Diaspora:
O'Donnell Lecture 17 November 2008

On 15 May 1959 the Taoiseach Eamon de Valera, asked Oscar Traynor, the Minister for Justice, to provide him with a certificate confirming that he was an Irish citizen. De Valera was a candidate for the presidency, and he wanted the certificate, in the event that he was challenged as to his eligibility to stand for election.[1] Eamon De Valera was born in New York, the son of an Irish emigrant woman, who worked as a domestic servant – a path followed by countless thousands of Irish female emigrants.[2] The fact that the most important political figure in the early decades of the Irish state was the son of an Irish emigrant is one indication of the centrality of emigration in the history of modern Ireland. There were, and are, few Irish families without direct experience of emigration. Although the Irish diaspora was dominated by labourers and domestic servants, it included doctors, nurses, engineers, school teachers, soldiers and businessmen; the NUI Club in London was for many years a popular meeting place for graduate emigrants.[3] Forty-one per cent of doctors who qualified in Ireland between 1850 and 1960 had careers overseas.[4] Nevertheless De Valera's story is unusual; Irish emigrants to the USA were less likely to return home, than emigrants from other European countries, and children of Irish emigrants were even less likely to settle in Ireland, though James Connolly, Jim Larkin and Desmond FitzGerald, (Minister for External Affairs in the Cosgrave government and father of NUI Chancellor Garret FitzGerald) are examples of this minority.

Eamon de Valera's close personal connections with the Irish diaspora are mentioned only in passing, if at all, in the standard histories of independent Ireland. I would suggest that one explanation for this surprising omission lies in the ambivalent attitude shown by the Irish state towards emigration and the wider Irish community overseas. This paper sets out to explore the relationship between the Irish state and the Irish diaspora.

[1] University College Dublin Archives, (UCDA) de Valera Papers, P150/3168 The Presidency, 15 May 1959 Eamon de Valera claimed Irish citizenship under the 1956 Irish nationality and citizenship act, which conferred citizenship by descent through the male or female line. He could have claimed Irish citizenship under article X of the 1922 Constitution, which gave Irish citizenship to those who were resident in Ireland on 6 December 1922 but that would have been contrary to his stance against the Anglo-Irish Treaty. For details of Irish nationality and citizenship legislation see Mary E. Daly, 'Irish nationality and citizenship since 1922', *Irish historical studies*, 32 no. 127, (May 2001), 377-407.

[2] Hasia Diner, *Erin's daughters in America:* Irish immigrant women in the nineteenth century, (Baltimore, 1983).

[3] The Club was founded in the 1920s by Irish professionals in London who found that they were not welcome in the traditional London club in the aftermath of the Anglo-Irish war. Tim Pat Coogan, *Wherever Green is Worn, The story of the Irish diaspora,* (London, 2000), 122.

[4] Greta Jones, '"Strike out boldly for the prizes that are available to you": medical emigration from Ireland 1860-1905, *Medical History,* 2010, vol 54, 55-74, Table 1, p.57 (forthcoming). My thanks to Professor Greta Jones for providing this information.

Some elements of this relationship feature prominently in the Irish media, notably the mass exodus of Irish government ministers to celebrate St. Patrick's Day around the world, and the US visitors and marching bands that travel to Ireland to march in St. Patrick's Day parades. Irish government ministers began to travel to Britain for St. Patrick's Day events in the 1930s; – the first Taoiseach to visit the White House on St. Patrick's Day was John A. Costello in 1956.[5] The international prominence given to the Northern Ireland question reflects the political and media influence of the Irish diaspora: while the Northern Ireland conflict destroyed families and communities, the 3,000 plus deaths are low on the scale of recent global tragedies, if compared with fatalities in Bosnia, or the conflicts in sub-Saharan Africa. Aspects of Irishness at home and abroad have been explored in the paintings of Sidney Nolan, the novels and short stories of Thomas Kennelly, Mary Gordon and William Kennedy, the plays of Eugene O'Neill and Martin McDonagh, and many other artists. The focus of this paper is more limited and less culturally enriching – how successive Irish governments and officials interacted with the Irish overseas.

The interaction was and remains a two-way process. A related story, but one that does not feature in this paper, would examine how the Irish overseas view the Irish state, and what demands, if any did they make on that state and its representatives? Chronology matters: the nature of the interaction between the Irish state and the Irish abroad changes over time. Finally, Ireland's relationship with the Irish diaspora should be seen as part of a modern global story: a case study in how the modern nation state relates to its citizens or potential citizens when they and their descendants live far beyond its borders, yet continue to claim an affiliation with the motherland, and what this relationship says about nationalism and the nation state.

To begin, we should address the term diaspora. Many scholars are uneasy about appropriating a word that is associated with the Shoah, and applying it to other ethnic groups. We could discuss this at length but I do not propose to do so. I am using the term diaspora because it captures some key themes: the continuing connection between Irish emigrants and their descendants with Ireland, and the recognition by the Irish state of a wider community overseas that is conscious of its Irish origins.[6] What is the connection between the 70m. people worldwide who identify in some way with Ireland and Irishness and the Irish state, and what does the Irish government mean when it acknowledges the 70m. Irish diaspora?[7]

[5] Mary E. Daly, 'Nationalism, sentiment, and economics: relations between Ireland and Irish America in the postwar world', in Kevin Kenny (ed.), *New directions in Irish-American history,* (Madison, Wisc., 2003), 264.

[6] Kevin Kenny, 'Diaspora and comparison: the global Irish as a case study', *Journal of American History,* 90 no. 1, (June 2003), 134-62; Stephane Dufoix, *Diasporas,* (translated William Rordarmor), (Berkeley, Cal, 2008).

[7] The 70m. figure is widely used, i.e. David McWilliams, i.e. 'Going tribal will save us from economic oblivion', *Irish Independent*, 18 March, 2009, and 'Diaspora can foster future success', *Irish Business Post*, 31 August, 2009. It is unclear how it has been determined. More than 40m. Americans claimed Irish ancestry in the 1990 census, but this fell to 30m. in 2000.

I

Mass emigration from Ireland predated the foundation of the state. By 1920 the great waves of emigration to North America and Australia had ended. The next wave, beginning in the late 1930s travelled to England. We hear a lot – quite rightly – about emigrants who were active in the cause for Irish independence, but much less about those who got on with their lives, whose links with Ireland were primarily personal: men and women who sent back remittances, and helped relatives and neighbours to emigrate. The key goal for most emigrants was to survive and improve their economic and social status in their new homes – these goals were assisted by a combination of community supports and assimilation into the new country. The primary support networks were family, neighbours, the Catholic Church – commonly staffed by Irish priests and nuns – and Irish voluntary associations. These networks predate Irish independence.

The Irish diaspora played a major role in the struggle for independence especially in the years after 1916 – they helped make it an international story that was covered by US media and press agencies.[8] The fledgling Irish foreign service drew on the Irish abroad from South Africa, to the Argentine, Australia to the USA, in their efforts to gain international recognition.[9] Dáil Éireann was largely reliant on funds collected in the USA. But de Valera's trip to the USA also reveals some key elements of the larger story. His relationship with Irish-American leaders was difficult, despite a common commitment to Irish independence. The divisions are sometimes presented as a clash of personalities; in reality they reflect different agendas.[10] De Valera's focus was on Ireland, whereas the Irish-American leadership was primarily concerned with domestic US politics. While Dáil Éireann was working to secure international recognition at the Paris Peace Conference and League of Nations, Irish-Americans were determined to keep the USA out of the League. Daniel Patrick Moynihan, one of the great writers on Irish America said that 'by 1916 Irish nationalism in America had little to do with Ireland. It was a hodgepodge of fine feeling and bad history with which the immigrants filled a cultural void'. Thomas N. Brown, one of the first scholars to tackle the topic of Irish-American nationalism, described Irish nationalism as 'the cement, not the purpose of Irish American organisations. Essentially they were pressure groups designed to defend and advance the

[8] Michael Doorley, *Irish-American diaspora nationalism.* The Friends of Irish Freedom, 1916-1935 (Dublin, 2005); Charles, Tansill, *America and the fight for Irish freedom, 1866-1922,* (New York, 1957).

[9] Ronan Fanning, Michael Kennedy, Dermot Keogh, Eunan O'Halpin (eds), *Documents on Irish foreign policy, vol I 1919-1922,* (Dublin, 1998).

[10] Doorley, *Irish-American diaspora nationalism,* 105-37; Kevin Kenny, 'American-Irish nationalism', in J. J. Lee and Marion R. Casey (eds), *Making the Irish American. History and heritage of the Irish in the United States,* (New York, 2006), 293-6.

American interests of the immigrant'.[11] Another lesson from this period is the transient affiliation of many emigrants with Irish causes. De Valera could attract 70,000 people to a rally in Boston's Fenway Park,[12] but in 1918, there were only 2,000 active members of the Friends of Irish Freedom.[13] Once the Treaty was signed, mass enthusiasm and mass involvement of Irish Americans with the Irish question faded away.

Many of the Irish overseas were enthusiastic about Irish independence, but that does not automatically translate into identification with the new state. Despite the strong theme of exile in Irish emigrant discourse very few returned to settle in Ireland after independence, and there was no effort to encourage them to do so. Veteran Fenian John Devoy remained in the USA, though he followed the tradition of former Fenians by being buried in Ireland with full ceremony, in his case a state funeral.[14]

As for the new state, from the beginning it trod a slippery line on emigration: deploring the practice, while not criticising individual emigrants, and reaching out to the Irish overseas. In the summer of 1920 the Dáil ministry drew up a proclamation banning emigration unless the intending emigrant secured the written sanction of the government of the Republic,which was duly approved by Dáil Éireann.[15] In April 1922 Minister for Home Affairs, Eamon Duggan reported that 1,578 of the 2,974 applications for emigration permits since June 1921 had been rejected; he believed that the process had reduced the number of emigrants.[16] Although there is no evidence that the Irish Free State continued to make emigration subject to official permit in later years, the Cosgrave government refused to sanction assisted emigration schemes to Canada or Australia during the 1920s, except for British ex-servicemen. Irish governments during the late 1940s and 1950s adopted a similar attitude, despite coming under sustained pressure from Irish-Australian catholic clergy and the Irish-Australian community who were keen to boost Irish immigration in the face of a rising inflow from southern Europe.[17] This is one of many instances where the agendas of the Irish government and the Irish overseas diverge. The standard rhetoric of successive governments, irrespective of party allegiance,

[11] Daniel Patrick Moynihan, 'The Irish' (1963,1970), reprinted in Lee and Casey (eds), *Making the Irish American,* 490. Thomas N. Brown, 'Social discrimination against the Irish in the United States. The American Jewish Committtee', November 1958 (mimeograph), 23 as cited by Moynihan, 490.

[12] Tim Pat Coogan, *De Valera: Long Fellow, Long Shadow,* (London, 1993), 150.

[13] Doorley, *Irish-American diaspora nationalism,* 87.

[14] Thomas J. Brophy, 'Political funerals and the realisation of Irish Independence, 1847-1929, PhD UCD 2004.

[15] Dáil Éireann, vol.I, 6 August 1920, cols 206-7. On 17 September the Secretary for Home Affairs reported that approximately 200 of the 250 applications for permits to emigrate had been approved because these applicants had booked passage before the decree was issued; he expected the approval rate to drop thereafter. Dáil Éireann, vol I, 17 September 1920, col.215.

[16] Dáil Éireann, vol. II, 26 April 1922, cols 240-41.

[17] Mary E. Daly, *The slow failure. Population decline and independent Ireland, 1920-1973,* (Madison, Wisc., 2006), 261-2.

was that the Irish state did not promote emigration – it was determined to create conditions that would make emigration unnecessary.[18]

But while deploring current emigration, Irish political leaders gloried in the diaspora. In 1948 during the debate on the Republic of Ireland Bill, John A. Costello, the then Taoiseach noted:

We are a small country. Our material wealth is comparatively insignificant, and we have no acquisitive or ambitions... Though we are a small nation, we wield an influence in the world far in excess of what our mere physical size and the smallness of our population might warrant. We are sometimes accused of acting as if we were a big nation. But, in fact we are a big nation. Our exiles have gone to practically every part of the world and have created for their motherland a spiritual dominion which more than compensates for her lack of size or material wealth. The Irish at home are only one section of a great race which has spread itself throughout the world, particularly in the great countries of North America and the Pacific area.[19]

Ireland's spiritual empire was commonly cited as the mirror image of Britain's material empire; those who used the term rarely reflected on Irish discomfort when Ireland was described as belonging to the British Empire or Commonwealth, or that the Australian Catholic Church might resent the dominant role played by Irish-born bishops.[20]

II

The new state made genuine efforts to engage with the wider Irish community. In 1926 W.T. Cosgrave made his first pre-recorded St. Patrick's Day broadcast to the USA, six years before King George V broadcast his first Christmas Day message.[21] The first live St. Patrick's Day message to the US went out in March 1931 – beginning a regular pattern. The 1931 broadcast appears to have attracted a large audience; it resulted in a flow of letters, Easter cards, and prayers sent to Mr. Cosgrave from Irish emigrants across the USA.[22] Nostalgia was a common theme in these addresses: Cosgrave's 1926 speech was a lyrical tour of Ireland – from the glens of Antrim to the Wicklow mountains, Killarney and the Rock of Cashel. The most famous St Patrick's Day broadcast is of course de Valera's 1943 account of 'the Ireland we have dreamed of'[23]. But the long-

[18] Daly, *The slow failure,* 144-5.

[19] Dáil Éireann, 24 November 1948, vol. 113, cols 392-3.

[20] 'Just as the Irish had argued that a predominantly Irish laity needed an Irish priesthood, so Australian priests now argued that a predominantly Australian laity needed an Australian priesthood. They argued that Irish clerical outlook was blind to Australia's real religious problems'. J.J. McGovern and Patrick J. O'Farrell, 'Australia, (ii) Development', Patrick O'Farrell, in Patrick Corish (ed.), *A history of Irish Catholicism,* vol. vi, no. 6. (Dublin, 1971), 73.

[21] National Archives Ireland, (NAI) Department of the Taoiseach files, S5111/1 Broadcast messages by the President. (Cosgrave was President of the Executive Council).

[22] NAI S5111/7, S5111/8

[23] For text of the speech see, Maurice Moynihan, *Speeches and statements by Eamon de Valera,* (Dublin, 1980), 466.

term potential of radio was not exploited. In 1946 the Radio Éireann budget was increased significantly in order to enable the station to set up a shortwave service targeted at the Irish overseas, and most especially at Irish-America, but the project was abandoned in 1948 by the incoming Inter-Party government. Although the plans were revived by the 1951-54 Fianna Fáil government, a regular shortwave station was never established.[24] As a consequence the Taoiseach's St. Patrick's Day message was transmitted on a number of occasions via the BBC world service.[25] When the Northern Ireland crisis exploded in the late 1960s, the government became concerned that it could not communicate their views on Northern Ireland to the Irish in Britain because Radio Teilfís Éireann (RTÉ) lacked the capacity to transmit either radio or television to Britain, but no steps were taken to rectify this shortcoming.[26] In recent years, although the internet has made Irish TV and radio available throughout the world, Irish emigrant groups have continued to lobby for a radio or television service that would reach the Irish in Britain. The 2006 Broadcasting Bill amended the public service remits of RTÉ and TG4 to make it possible to allocate money from the Irish television licence to provide such a service.[27] Plans were drawn up for Diaspora TV, which would transmit programmes from the RTÉ channels and TG4, including live news bulletins, to the UK. But the service, which was scheduled to commence on St. Patrick's Day 2009, has been postponed – a casualty of the 2008 recession,[28] raising memories of the ill-fated short-wave radio station.

III

Irish citizenship offered both a means of connecting with the Irish abroad, and as Terence O'Neill, onetime prime minister of Northern Ireland suggested rather maliciously – a way to compensate for the decline in the numbers who were resident in the state.[29] Under the 1935 Irish Nationality and Citizenship Act, emigrants born in Ireland, or with a father or paternal grandfather of Irish birth, could apply for Irish citizenship. The Act was deliberately framed to replicate the British Nationality Act; it was part of de Valera's strategy of maximising Irish independence within the Commonwealth, while avoiding a formal breach. For this reason the act did not provide for citizenship by descent through the female line – though de Valera expressed personal regrets over this, (with good reason). When the act was passed Irish politicians expressed the hope that Irish people

[24] Maurice Gorham, *Forty years of Irish broadcasting,* (Dublin, 1967), 152-61.There were technical difficulties with respect to wavelength and Gorham notes (158) that few Americans used short-wave radio.

[25] Gorham, *Forty Years of Irish Broadcasting,* 199.

[26] National Archives Ireland, Department of the Taoiseach files, 2000/6/553 Radio Teilfís Éireann reception in Six Counties (Northern Ireland) and Britain. August 1969-October 1970.

[27] Dáil Debates, vol. 631, 14 February 2007, col. 1316.

[28] Press Release, Department of Communications, Energy and Natural Resources, 17 March 2008; *Irish Independent,* 6 November 2008.

[29] Daly, 'Irish nationality and citizenship', 403. O'Neill's comments were prompted by the introduction of the bill that became the 1956 Irish Nationality and Citizenship Act.

throughout the world would take out citizenship. Some took up the offer – George Bernard Shaw and his wife Charlotte, who were resident in London; Loreto sisters in Spain and South America; Irish emigrants in the USA, including some oil workers from Texas and Pennsylvania coalminers. The majority of US applicants for citizenship were women, many old and seemingly poor, with addresses in nursing homes and boarding houses; some women applicants were domestic servants with addresses on the best streets in Manhattan. The 1956 Act extended citizenship by descent to the female line, and made it easier to claim citizenship. During the debate several TDs again expressed hopes that descendants of emigrants would settle in Ireland. But throughout the 1950s fewer than 100 people a year with overseas addresses claimed citizenship. In the 50 years from 1936 to 1986 only 16,500 people claimed citizenship by descent. The majority of these applied in the 1980s, when the benefits of an Irish passport were becoming evident: it conveyed the freedom to work and move throughout the European Union and, more importantly the right to live and work in Britain. This proved particularly attractive to citizens of Australia, Canada, and former British colonies in Africa who had lost residency rights under the UK Commonwealth Immigration Acts. The major beneficiaries were residents of South Africa, Zimbabwe and former British colonies in Africa, who account for over 44 per cent of successful applicants – though Irish emigrants to Africa were a tiny minority of the total.[30] This suggests that applications for Irish citizenship had little to do with sentiment. This is not surprising. Until recent times, dual citizenship was anathema in international law. In the 1930s the League of Nations stated that everybody was entitled to one nationality, nobody should have two. For a US resident opting for Irish citizenship would preclude them from becoming a policeman, public school teacher or holding any government position. In the highly nativist atmosphere of the 1930s continuing to hold Irish rather than US citizenship would have not been a wise move. Moreover, Irish citizens could not vote. Irish-American political leaders went to considerable efforts to fast-track US citizenship for Irish emigrants, in order to maximise their electoral advantage. In 1940 Irish-born emigrants had the highest rate of naturalisation of all emigrant groups in major US cities.[31] A much higher proportion of Italian emigrants retained Italian citizenship, but many returned to settle in Italy, and, in contrast to Ireland, the Italian state provided assistance for emigrants in need.

When Irish emigrants landed in Cobh brandishing a US passport they got a less than wonderful welcome – there are some heartrending letters from men and women, born in Ireland, who were told by Irish immigration officers that they could only stay six weeks or three months. Although de Valera intervened to moderate the policies of the Department

[30] Further details re the above and succeeding paragraphs can be found in Daly, 'Irish nationality and citizenship'.

[31] Matthew J. O'Brien, 'Transatlantic connections and the sharp edge of the Great Depression', in Kenny (ed.), *New directions in Irish-American history,* 87-88.

of Justice, ensuring that returning emigrants who wished to remain could settle permanently in Ireland, regardless of the passport that they carried, the official policy was not welcoming.[32] For those living overseas with an Irish passport, official parsimony meant a scant network of embassies and consulates; so that Irish emigrants often had to rely on UK consulates for assistance, which might be problematic. When the Irish Franciscans in Rome were faced with losing their garden to a major road scheme they appealed to W.T. Cosgrave for assistance, but they also appealed to the British Minister in Rome.[33] They were probably not alone in hedging their bets.

IV

The Irish government record on protecting emigrants' rights was patchy. In the 1920s the Irish Minister in Washington, T.J. Smiddy, successfully negotiated a short-term increase in the number of emigrant visas allocated to the Irish Free State (it expired in 1929).[34] When war broke out in 1939 the Irish authorities secured agreement that Irish emigrants could work in Britain for two years without becoming subject to conscription. Indeed despite repeated statements that they would do nothing to promote emigration, throughout World War II, the Irish authorities actively co-operated in organising Irish emigration to Britain; Irish Labour Exchanges were used by British recruiters. Were all interests served by this? Probably. Emigration reduced the numbers of unemployed in Ireland; many families were fed by emigrants' remittances, easing the burden on the Irish taxpayer. Indeed the real fears within Irish government circles were of a sudden return home when the war ended; the servant crisis suffered by Dublin middle-class families was another minor irritant.[35]

From the late 1930s, until the mid-'60s, there were intermittent demands in Britain for restrictions to be imposed on immigration from Ireland. At such times the Irish authorities generally stayed silent and hoped that Britain's economic interests would prevail and controls would not be applied – the strategy proved to be correct, but it was a close-run thing. Costello's announcement in 1948 that Ireland would declare a Republic and leave the commonwealth was made without due consideration for the status of the Irish in Britain, and it gave rise to panic within the Irish community. All was well – thanks to Britain's continuing need for Irish workers and the support of commonwealth nations; the Irish diaspora in Australia and other commonwealth countries proved an important lobby preventing Britain from retaliating against Ireland.[36] Controls on Irish immigrants could

[32] Daly, 'Irish nationality and citizenship', 395-7.

[33] Mary E. Daly, 'A second golden age: the Irish Franciscans 1919-1963', in Edel Bhreathnach, Joseph MacMahon & John McCafferty, *The Irish Franciscans 1540-1990,* (Dublin, 2009 forthcoming),

[34] NAI, Department of the Taoiseach S3292

[35] Daly, *The slow failure,* 144-51.

[36] Daly, 'Irish nationality and citizenship', 390; Ian McCabe, *A diplomatic history of Ireland, 1948-49,* (Dublin, 1991), 37,58-9,79,83.

well have been introduced as part of the 1963 Commonwealth Immigration Act. They were probably averted because partition meant that they would be unenforceable unless the documents of all travellers to Britain from Northern Ireland were checked. But the Irish authorities made little effort to prevent Irish emigrants being conscripted into the US armed forces, despite an agreement signed in 1950 that this would not happen.[37]

Over 400,000 Irish men and women emigrated to Britain from the late 1940s to the mid 1960s, but no consideration was given to opening consular offices to cater for their needs.[38] When ten migrant tatiehokers from Achill – aged from 13 to 23 years – died in a bothy fire in Scotland in 1937, Minister for Justice PJ. Ruttledge, who happened to be in London for a St. Patrick's Day dinner, travelled to Scotland, and arranged for the bodies to be brought home, but the dominant reaction in the Department of External Affairs was concern at how the story would be presented in Britain. Officials expressed fears that the inquest would determine that they had been drinking (they hadn't), or that the tragedy would provoke anti-Irish feeling in Britain.[39] Irish potato pickers were still living and working in appalling conditions in the late 1960s – but the Irish authorities remained reluctant to intervene.[40]

Among the thousands of navvies, nurses, and factory labourers travelling to Britain there was a steady stream of pregnant single women: British welfare services classified them as PFI – pregnant from Ireland. Many girls and boys in their early teens arrived in Britain with little money and no contacts, often leaving Ireland with parental permission even persuasion, in the expectation that they would send money home. Responsibility for looking after these vulnerable groups, and caring for Irish ex-prisoners and the many former inmates of Irish industrial schools who settled in Britain, fell on British local authorities, and Catholic charities. The charities often appealed to Dublin for assistance. First port of call was generally the Dublin archdiocese, soon followed by a visit to Iveagh House or letters to the Taoiseach. The exchanges on these issues were rarely flattering to the Irish; some British Catholic charity workers – especially those associated with the archdiocese of Westminster – adopted a patronising tone that disparaged the moral and religious values of Irish emigrants. But Irish assistance to emigrants in need was almost non-existent. Girls proven to have become pregnant in Ireland were repatriated at state expense to a mother and baby home in Cork; the rest became a charge on British

[37] NAI, DFA Washington Files, D23. Visit to the USA by Seán Lemasss 1953.

[38] The Department of External Affairs (now Foreign Affairs) took a conscious decision not to provide consular services to the Irish in Britain, because they feared that doing so would jeopardise the status of the Irish in Britain; providing consular services would be tantamount to acknowledging that the Irish in Britain were foreigners. I am grateful to the Irish Abroad unit in the Department of Foreign Affairs for this observation.

[39] Daly, *The slow failure,* 266-9.

[40] Dáil Debates, vol. 191, 3 August 1961, col. 3. Heather Holmes, 'Sanitary inspectors and the reform of housing conditions for Irish migratory potato workers in Scotland from 1945 to the 1970s', *Saothar,* 24, (1999), 45-58.

charities.[41] Only in the 1960s did Irish consulates begin to pay return travel costs for citizens in difficulty, and the scheme was primarily designed to assist stranded tourists, not emigrants.

V

There were several flash-points over the welfare of the Irish in Britain – one came in 1951 when Eamon de Valera received a report on living conditions of Irish emigrants in the Midlands, written by Maurice Foley, then a Catholic social worker, later a British Labour MP and Minister in Harold Wilson's government. De Valera employed Foley's graphic descriptions of twenty Irish emigrants sharing one bed room; groups of men and women sharing bedrooms – the women sleeping there at night, the men during the day, and other vignettes as the basis for a carefully-flagged speech at a Fianna Fáil dinner in Galway; though he omitted Foley's descriptions of teenage pregnancies, alcohol abuse, and married male emigrants with second families in Britain. The speech was reported in all leading British newspapers. (media calls were handled by a young diplomat called Conor Cruise O'Brien).[42] De Valera had no qualms about describing the misery of the emigrant's life to drive home his message, that they would have a better quality of life, both materially and personally, if they had remained in Ireland. While de Valera may have wished to deter would-be emigrants, his speech showed little regard for the Irish in Britain. Many were outraged by the speech; some claimed that it left them open to taunts at work. Others drew attention to the overcrowded slum housing in central Dublin within walking distance of Dáil Éireann.[43]

Foley's report was an attempt to persuade the Irish government to provide welfare services for emigrants – it did not succeed. Successive ministers for External/Foreign Affairs in the 1950s, 60s and 70s argued that welfare support would only encourage emigration, which was contrary to government policy; that Britain was more prosperous, and had superior welfare services to Ireland – the Irish in Britain had higher average earnings than the Irish at home – so why should they be subsidised? They even suggested that the Irish government was being asked to subsidise welfare services provided by the Catholic church, going on to argue that the state could not assist such denominationally-based services – an argument that conveniently forgets the substantial financial support given to hospitals, care homes and other institutions in Ireland. On a number of occasions the London embassy expressed concern that Irish emigrants were sharing lodgings with coloured immigrants; they were also worried about Communist tendencies in groups such as the Connolly Clubs, but they were prepared to leave it to

[41] Lindsey Earner-Byrne, 'The boat to England: an analysis of the official reactions to the emigration of single expectant Irishwomen to Britain 1922-1972', *Irish economic and social history,* 30 (2003), 52-70; Daly *The slow failure,* 256-96.

[42] Daly, *The slow failure,* 270-76.

[43] NAI, DT, S11582C.

the Catholic church, Irish emigrant groups and British local authorities to meet emigrants' needs.[44] The Irish Centre in Camden town was built with money from the Irish hierarchy, and local fundraising, and there were countless appeals to Dublin for assistance. But despite repeated visits to the Centre by successive Irish ambassadors to the UK and visiting Cabinet ministers, this support was not forthcoming.[45] Irish Centres in Birmingham, Manchester and elsewhere were likewise financed by local Irish communities – who were simultaneously struggling to provide Catholic schools and larger churches to cope with the Irish influx. Admittedly arguments about emigrant welfare were enveloped in moral and religious issues: pregnancies out of wedlock, marital infidelity or non-attendance at church. There were also tensions in the 1950s between the Irish embassy and the Catholic Church; the embassy was keen to see emigrants dispersed and thus less visible in English cities, rather than congregated in Irish communities; whereas the church wanted to keep them together in the hope that this would improve the prospects that they would continue to practice their religion.

The Irish and English hierarchies also disagreed over the respective merits of assimilating Irish emigrants, or continuing to regard them as a distinct category. The Irish hierarchy wanted Irish priests ministering to the Irish, and missions by Irish clergy targeting the Irish; the English church preferred integrated missions.[46] But there was little appreciation in Ireland of the cost that 1950s immigration imposed on British Catholicism – something that is easier to comprehend today when we see the pressures that recent immigration has placed on Irish schools and social services.

VI

Irish-American neighbourhoods were more mature and settled entities; they were not forced to confront a large influx of new arrivals. Furthermore high-risk and vulnerable immigrants, such as runaway teenagers and pregnant women were unlikely to obtain US visas. But in the USA as in Britain the burden of emigrant welfare and the provision of social spaces fell on the Catholic church and voluntary groups. In 1954 Paul Keating, Irish Consul General in New York, noted that the consulate made no effort to get in touch with the Irish community. 'Generally speaking we are embarrassed by callers who have nothing to recommend them except their Irish citizenship... We cannot afford to entertain them... we do not even have a St. Patrick's Day reception for Irish citizens'.[47] In the 1930s de Valera contacted Eoin MacNeill, chairman of the Irish Manuscripts Commission, to explore the possibility of establishing Irish libraries throughout the US – modelled on the American Scandinavian Foundation. The concept was the brainchild of

[44] Daly, *The slow failure,* 289-328.

[45] Gerry Harrison, *The Scattering. A history of the London Irish Centre, 1954-2004,* (London, 2004).

[46] Daly, *The slow failure,* 304-7. A.E.C.W. Spencer, 'The religious arrangements for the integration of Irish Catholic immigrants in England and Wales', Unpublished report, 1959, Dublin Diocesan Archives.

[47] NAI, Department of Foreign Affairs (DFA) Washington Embassy, P115/1, 23 July 1954.

the writer Felix Hackett, who was keen to establish an annual colloquium in Ireland to educate Irish Americans about Ireland. Hackett also wanted to send young Irish graduates to the USA to learn something of the problems and mental outlook of the American-Irish.[48] But nothing happened. Irish culture overseas was more likely to be sustained by Comhaltas Ceoltóirí, the GAA, and by Catholic schools. But whereas Catholic schools in North America and Australia promoted Irish culture and an Irish identity, with the assistance of Irish-born lay and religious teachers, in Britain, according to Mary Hickman this was not so. British Catholic schools 'aimed at neutralizing the political identity of second-generation Irish children as Irish by strengthening their Catholic identity... In this process the Irishness or Irish heritage of Catholic working-class communities was effectively rendered invisible.'[49] In the early decades of the twentieth century, the US university that made the greatest contribution to Irish scholarship was Harvard – they promoted major anthropological and archaeological studies in the 1930s in partnership with the Irish state – but there were few Irish-American students at Harvard at the time.[50] US Catholic colleges were so determined to promote integration and upward mobility for US Catholics that Irish history and culture did not figure on the curriculum. This has changed in recent decades, now that the economic and social success of US Catholics has been assured.[51]

VII

The most active engagement between Ireland and the diaspora in the decades after independence revolved around the anti-partition campaign. In 1949 the all-party Mansion House committee launched a drive to end partition. De Valera, who was out of office, embarked on a round the world anti-partition tour – drawing large crowds in North America, Australia and Britain, though John Bowman claims – probably correctly – that he was speaking to the converted.[52] The anti-partition campaign continued to make noise in the USA throughout the '50s – there were congressional resolutions, and Irish American groups distributed anti-partition literature.[53] But Irish-Americans criticised recent emigrants for their lack of commitment to the anti-partition cause.[54] The Irish in

[48] NAI, Department of the Taoiseach, S9215A, Irish-American cultural foundation.

[49] Mary Hickman, *Religion, class and identity. The state, the Catholic Church and the education of the Irish in Britain,* (Aldershot, 1995), 203-4.

[50] Anne Byrne, Ricca Edmondson and Tony Varley, Introduction to Conrad M. Arensberg and Solon T. Kimball, *Family and community in Ireland,* third edition, Ennis, 2001, xvii-lxix; Daly, *The slow failure,* 81-2; Mairead Carew, IRCHSS Ph.D. scholar is currently researching the impact of the Harvard excavations on Irish archaeology

[51] J.J.Lee, 'Introduction: reinterpreting Irish America', in Lee and Casey (eds), *Making the Irish American,* 44-48.

[52] John Bowman, *De Valera and the Ulster question, 1917-1973,* (Oxford), 274.

[53] Sean Cronin, *Washington's Irish policy 1916-1986: Independence, Partition, Neutrality,* (Dublin, 1987), 194, 274-5.

[54] NAI, DFA, Washington Embassy P 115/1, Irish ambassador to the USA Joseph Brennan to Pat Hughes, Irish Consul, San Francisco, 15 July 1954.

Britain appear to have been even less enthusiastic – not surprising, because an active anti-partition campaign would have ignited the low level anti-Irish feeling that existed. Nevertheless throughout the 1950s the contribution that the Irish community in Britain might make to the anti-partition campaign was of greater interest to the Department of Foreign Affairs than their material conditions.[55]

VIII

Emigrants' remittances were a more personal form of connection between the Irish overseas and those at home, but one that was of major importance to the Irish economy. Emigrants' remittances were the largest source of dollar earnings until the late 1950s.[56] Data on remittances from Britain is less reliable, because most of the money arrived in personal letters and British bank-notes were interchangeable with Irish currency, but they were undoubtedly significant. By the early 1950s with the dollar the world's most sought-after currency, a tourism drive targeted at Irish-America offered economic benefits and a means for reconnecting with the Irish diaspora. The marketing plan drawn up by Pan American airlines targeting the 20 million Americans of Irish ancestry provided the template for subsequent Irish tourist programmes. Pan-Am suggested that Ireland should recognise the overseas Irish and their contribution to advancing the prestige of the Irish people: March would be 'Come Back to Erin Month'; the festival – An Tóstal would be marketed using the slogan – 'Ireland at home'. Plans included a register of all Irish overseas; children could be enrolled at birth on a scroll in the National Museum. They also proposed a beauty contest to choose a 'typical Irish colleen' – someone like the successful Hollywood movie-stars, Maureen O'Hara and Maureen O'Sullivan; an Irish heritage centre – mapping family origins and a theme park 'The Valley of the Fairies or the home of the Leprachauns', complete with tiny footprints.[57]

Seán Lemass (Minister for Industry and Commerce), vetoed the 'Valley of the Fairies' and tensions soon emerged between economic goals and sentimental reconnection. Returning emigrants stayed with relatives and made a modest contribution to foreign exchange. The high spenders were third or fourth generation Irish-Americans. There were also tensions between Pan-American airlines' ambition for direct flights into Dublin and the Irish government's determination to promote Shannon airport.[58] Nevertheless ethnic tourism prospered especially in the 1960s, giving rise to medieval banquets, CIÉ coach-tours, mass sales of Waterford glass and other cultural innovations, including the Rose of Tralee, a beauty contest that targeted the Irish communities worldwide.

[55] Enda Delaney, *The Irish in post-war Britain,* (Oxford, 2006), 186-9.

[56] In 1957 emigrants remittances from the dollar area were valued at £6.2m.; merchandise exports to the dollar area were valued at £4.04m. Statistical Abstract 1958.

[57] Irene Furlong, *Irish tourism, 1880-1980,* (Dublin, 2009), 168-76.

[58] Daly, 'Nationalism, sentiment and economics', 266-9.

IX

The 1960s is a transition period. By the early sixties Lemass and his ministers were of the opinion that mass emigration was at an end. Against the background of improving relations with Britain, Donogh O'Malley (Minister for Health), told a 1966 St. Patrick's Day gathering at the NUI Club in London that the Irish in Britain should reject 'maudlin sentimentality about "the old country" and seek to play a full part in British political and social life'.[59] This message may reflect O'Malley's assessment of the economic potential of the Irish diaspora, carried out as a by-product of the First Programme for Economic Expansion, which came to the conclusion that Irish ethnic networks – in Britain, Canada, Australia and the USA were of limited economic value except to tourism. The political influence of Irish-America was seen as declining; their interest in Ireland 'limited to a sentimental regard for their ancestry, which does not involve financial expenditure'.[60]

Partition gradually faded even from political speeches, though in 1963, on the eve of John F. Kennedy's visit to Ireland, T.J. Kiernan, Irish ambassador in the US was asked to broach the possibility that the President would urge the British authorities to make a public statement indicating that a solution to partition was in the best interests of Britain and Ireland. Kennedy's response was that no British minister would feel able to make such a statement in public; a better approach would be to encourage an atmosphere in Belfast that would favour closer relations between the two parts of Ireland[61] – an approach that was consistent with Lemass' policy at the time.

When Lemass visited the USA in the autumn of 1963, shortly after Kennedy's triumphant visit to Ireland, he expressed hopes that 'the miracle of modern travel and mass communications' would reverse the growing separation between Ireland and the Irish overseas; he also noted that for the first time in history 'The Irish Nation at home and the Irish race abroad' were experiencing common feelings of success and progress. Lemass wanted to build on that success by establishing an Irish-American Foundation to promote Irish history and literature; more controversially he suggested that Irish Societies which looked after the interests of Irish-Americans should turn their attention to Ireland, now that Irish-America was prosperous and secure.[62] But a report by senior civil servants on proposals for an Irish Chamber of Commerce in the United States decided that it should not become an Irish-American organisation, but a group consisting of heads of major US businesses; no ethnic Irish connections were necessary for membership.[63]

[59] Delany *The Irish in post-war Britain,* 179-80, 204.

[60] NAI DFA P115/1, 27 June 1958;

[61] NAI Department of the Taoiseach S17401B President Kennedy's visit to Ireland 19 March 1963. Cable from Kiernan to Hugh McCann, Secretary Department External Affairs.

[62] NAI Department of the Taoiseach S17400C Sean Lemass's visit to USA; speech to Irish Societies in Boston,

[63] NAI DT S9215/B/62.

The proposed Irish-American Cultural Foundation likewise targeted wealthy Americans – Irish ancestry was regarded as optional.

By the 1960s Lemass and Irish officials were keen to boost Ireland's international standing, and to promote the image of a prosperous modern nation. This goal was best served by targeting wealthier people, whose ethnic connections with Ireland were lost in the mists of time, and Irish-Americans who had migrated to the suburbs away from than the traditional ethnic communities, which were still dominated by blue collar and lower middle class occupations. Many of the latter were unhappy about Ireland's improved relations with Britain and the government of Northern Ireland, and the Irish government's abandoning of the anti-partition rhetoric. When Lemass visited Chicago in 1963 Irish diplomats urged him to at least mention partition because the audience would expect it.[64] The unhappiness of Irish-American groups at the Irish government's new policy towards Northern Ireland resurfaced during celebrations marking the Golden Jubilee of the 1916 Rising. The Irish consul-general in New York reported that he attended a special mass to commemorate 1916 but he absented himself from the memorial parade organised by the Associated Irish Societies, where various IRA veterans were given a prominent role and from the dinner hosted by the Ancient Order of Hibernians.[65] Further evidence of the growing distance between the Irish government and Irish-American communities comes in the relaxed attitude that Ireland adopted towards the 1965 reform of US immigration law. One Irish diplomat suggested that the loss of Ireland's national quota would cause no great difficulties because Irish immigrants were well-educated, spoke English and had relatives in the USA, and would therefore continue to find it easy to emigrate to the USA. The reality proved rather different – most would-be emigrants had only primary schooling, and their American relatives were increasingly distant cousins. Irish immigration had plummeted by the end of the decade, and protests from south Boston began to reach Irish diplomats.[66]

X

The outbreak of violence in Northern Ireland in 1969 prompted serious reconsideration of the Irish government's relationship with the Irish abroad. This is the best-known part of the story, so my treatment will be brief.[67] Irish authorities had to work to create a third way – between Irish immigrant groups speaking and working on behalf of the IRA, and the powerful British presence in media and diplomatic circles. Irish diplomats based in the USA engaged with the Irish American community as never before to build a coalition

64 NAI DFA 22/1 Washington Embassy.

65 NAI DFA Washington Embassy 2201/37/781/P153 II 50th Anniversary of the Easter Rising.

66 NAI DFA Washington Embassy C60, Irish immigration.

67 Andrew J. Wilson, *Irish America and the Ulster Conflict 1968-1985,* (Belfast, 1995); Conor O'Clery, *The greening of the White House* (Dublin, 1996).

of Irish-American interests aligned with Irish government policy. The Ireland Fund, Irish-American partnership, and other elite groups enlisted the 'soft power' and financial assistance of wealthy Irish-Americans.[68] Irish diplomats like Sean Donlon and Michael Lillis forged close links with Irish-American politicians to influence the Irish policy of Presidents Carter and Reagan, and to deploy US presidential influence on Margaret Thatcher.[69] In Britain the challenge of the Northern Ireland crisis decades was even greater, though it is not as well documented. IRA bombing incidents in Britain, the jailing of the Birmingham Six and the Guildford Four, and the searches and security surveillance, shattered the Irish community. But they also resulted in new contact between Irish politicians and the Irish in Britain. Visits by Irish politicians to the imprisoned Birmingham Six and other political prisoner, which were often initiated by TDs rather than government ministers, and campaigns for their release created an awareness of other less high-profile Irish prisoners in Britain.[70] Irish diplomats now routinely visit Irish prisoners in Britain and work with their families.

The 1980s wave of emigration to Britain and the USA also changed the agenda. While 1950s Irish emigrants were often bitter at having to leave Ireland they made no concerted effort to put pressure on the Irish government to provide assistance.[71] The 1980s generation was more assertive. Mary Corcoran points out that the '1980s generation had expected a good living in Ireland - when it did not materialise they went, but not quietly – they campaigned for what they saw as their rights, and were forthright in criticism of the Irish government'.[72] Linda Almeida Dowling noted that 'when Irish journalists broadcast the problems of Irish illegal aliens, a sense of Irish entitlement in America permeated the stories. Despite the fact that the undocumented Irish broke U.S. immigration laws, the reports emphasized the rights of the Irish to better treatment because of Ireland's long immigrant tradition in America'.[73] This emigrant generation also received much wider media coverage in Ireland and overseas than earlier generations.[74] They remained in closer contact with home by phone or return visits; many saw their stay overseas as temporary. Irish emigrants were free to move within the European Union, but the majority of emigrants to the USA worked illegally. The discord and generation gap between established Irish-America and the new Irish immigrants was also noticeable.[75] When the 1986 USA Immigration Reform and Control Act made it much

[68] Wilson, *Irish America and the Ulster conflict,* 121-4.

[69] Wilson, *Irish America and the Ulster conflict,* 126-67, 180, 194, 238-50; Garret FitzGerald, *All in a Life,* (Dublin, 1991), 348-9.

[70] David Andrews, *Kingstown Republican. A memoir,* (Dublin, 2007), 107-30.

[71] A number of anti-emigration groups were established in Ireland during the 1950s but they had limited impact. Daly, *The slow failure,* 203-5.

[72] Mary P. Corcoran, *Irish Illegals. Transients between two societies,* (Westport, Conn., 1993), 34, 116-7.

[73] Linda Dowling Almeida, *Irish immigrants in New York City 1945-1996* (Bloomington, Indiana, 2001), 4.

[74] Corcoran, *Irish Illegals,* 49-51.

[75] Corcoran *Irish Illegals,* 126-32; Almeida, *Irish immigrants in New York City,* 74.

more difficult for illegal immigrants to survive in the USA, they founded the Irish Immigration Reform Movement, a support group to help with jobs and welfare, and a lobby group; this role was later taken over by the Emigrant Isle Immigration Society . These societies tapped into the Irish-American political networks that had evolved to deal with Northern Ireland, and they demanded assistance from the Irish government. One New York priest working with the undocumented Irish complained about the 'stand-offish attitude' of the Irish consulate towards the new wave of immigrants. This changed in 1987 when Minister for Foreign Affairs, Brian Lenihan appointed the first immigrant liaison officer at the New York consulate.[76]

The impact of the 1980s emigrants is evident both in the Donnelly and Morrison US visa programmes, and in the campaigns in Ireland for votes for emigrants. The 1992 proposal for a partnership government between Fianna Fáil and the Progressive Democrats accepted the principal that the constitution should be amended to give votes to emigrants in Senate, Europe and Presidential elections;[77] but in 1996 the subsequent Fine Gael-Labour coalition decided not to proceed with this measure given the 'divergence of views' on the matter. Five groups campaigning for voting rights for emigrants 'expressed varying degrees of opposition to Seanad representation for emigrants, even as a full step towards full voting rights'; other emigrant organisations were likewise divided on the matter.[78] But Mary Robinson's speech to the joint houses of the Oireachtas in February 1995 [79] – the first by an Irish President (US President John F Kennedy addressed a joint sitting of the Oireachtas in 1963) – reflected the new visibility of the Irish diaspora, as did the strong focus on emigration during the 1995-97 commemoration of the sesquicentenary of the great famine.[80] The formation of an Irish Abroad Unit in Iveagh House and recent Irish government funding for Irish language studies in Notre Dame, and chairs in Cambridge and Liverpool – are indications that this is a dynamic and rapidly-changing story.

XI

For most of the past eighty years or so since independence, Ireland and the Irish diaspora have operated as independent communities that interacted, perhaps collided occasionally. It is possible to read at length about the history of independent Ireland and learn nothing about the Irish diaspora, and the most salient feature of the many histories of Irish communities overseas is the absence of anything other than the most cursory references to recent Irish history. The relationship between Ireland and those living and

[76] Almeida, *Irish Immigrants in New York City,* 103.

[77] Dáil Éireann, vol 431 19 May 1993, Minister for the Environment, M. Smith, col. 100.

[78] Dáil Éireann, vol. 471, 13 Nov. 1996, Written answers, voting rights for emigrants, Minister for State at the Dept. of the Environment, Mr Allen, col 1022; Seanad Éireann, vol.148, 10 October 1996, cols.1606-7.

[79] Dáil Éireann, vol. 448, 2 Feb. 1995, Address by Uachtarán na hÉireann to Joint Sitting of the Houses of the Oireachtas, cols. 1145-56.

[80] This was emphasised in the 1995 address to the Oireachtas by President Robinson.

perhaps born overseas who identify with Ireland has commonly been characterised by lack of mutual understanding, and by a mutual failure to recognise what President Mary McAleese described as 'the subtleties and complexities around the nature of the Irish Diaspora'.[81] It is foolhardy to make generalizations about a diverse group of 80 million, that includes those of Irish birth, who have been resident in Britain for fifty years; Australian citizens with one grandparent or great-grandparent who was born in Ireland, with the remainder of British, Italian or Greek ancestry; South African-born Irish passport holders happily resident in Britain who may never have visited Ireland but were fortunate to have a grandparent born in Ireland, and Americans who claim an ancestor who is believed to have fled Ireland during the famine.

Interest in ethnic origins and identification with ethnic communities has grown rapidly in recent years. It is a product of global travel and new digital media. The interest is strengthened by the fashion for tracing family origins – evident in programmes such as 'Who do you think you are'. In many ways this renewed interest in ethnic origins is a consequence of the mobility and lack of geographical and community roots that characterises contemporary societies; it may reflect a search for a more stable past, however fanciful, in today's transient and mobile environment. The renewed interest in the mother country has promoted new efforts by Ireland to connect with this diaspora. This too is a global phenomenon – replicated by other countries with large expatriate communities. Italy introduced votes for immigrants in 2001.[82] Greece has a Council of Greeks Abroad. India has sought through special tax treatment to use the Indian diaspora to drive economic development at home.[83] Italy, like Ireland has strengthened its national soccer squad by drawing on Italian emigrant communities.[84] Croatia and Iraq are among the many countries where diasporic communities have tried to influence domestic political agendas; Greece tried to enlist the Greek communities overseas, especially those in the USA in support of the Greek-Cpriot campaign following the 1974 Turkish invasion of northern Cyprus;[85] China has created an overseas Chinese museum and a World Overseas Chinese Cemetery.[86] Expatriate identification with Ireland, Italy or any mother

[81] In a speech to the Second UCD Irish Diaspora Forum in the UCD John Home Global Irish Institute, 10 November 2008.

[82] Ferruccio Pastore, 'A community out of balance: nationality law and migration politics in the history of post-unification Italy', *Journal of modern Italian studies,* vol. 9, no. 1, 2004, 35.

[83] Marie, Lall, 'Mother India's forgotten children', in Eva Østergaard-Nielsen (ed.) *International migration and sending countries. Perceptions, policies and transnational relations,* (London, 2003), 121-39.

[84] 35 Pastore, 'A community out of balance', 35.

[85] George Prevlakis, '*Finis Greciae* or the return of the Greeks? State and diaspora in the context of globalisation', Talk given in the seminar series 'Globalisation and the "Old" Diasporas', organised by the Transnational Communities Programme at the School of Geography, University of Oxford, 12 November 1998.

[86] Eva Østergaard-Nielsen, 'International migration and sending countries: key issues and themes' in Østergaard-Nielsen (ed.) *International migration and sending countries. Perceptions, policies and transnational relations,* 17.

country is volatile; the numbers claiming Irish ancestry in the US census fell from 40m in 1990 to 34.5m in 2000.

The decision to identify with Ireland, and how this global community identifies with Ireland is determined in part by what it means to be an Australian, British or US citizen, and how Ireland is perceived. The end of violence in Northern Ireland and Ireland's economic success made it easier for British residents of Irish birth or descent to publicly identify with Ireland, and this identification with Ireland also reflects a fragmenting of Britishness with the rise of Scottish, Welsh or English identities. A diaspora is always characterised by hybrid identities. But in a hybrid national identity which has priority, which carries the greater responsibility? Ireland is now what is termed a receiving state. There are churches in Ireland that cater almost exclusively for Polish or Nigerian communities; shops and other services with a strong ethnic focus. A number of Irish primary and secondary schools now have to decide how to balance the need to preserve a migrant child's ethnic identity, while making them aware of Ireland and its history and traditions. The emergence of these diasporic communities in Ireland, with their complex and sometimes contradictory loyalties and identities should help to promote greater awareness of the forms of loyalties and identities that result from migration beyond the nation state. These 'new Irish', and the Irish diaspora reflect a world where the boundaries of the nation state are increasingly blurred, with a growing number of people claiming hybrid and trans-national identities. This presents a challenge for the Irish state, and for many other nation states in the twenty-first century.[87]

[87] Donna Gabaccia, 'Italian history and gli Italiani nel mondo, Part II. *Journal of modern Italian studies,* vol 3, no. 1 (1998), 73-97.